# GODS & GODDESSES
## OF THE ANCIENT WORLD

# Anubis

BY VIRGINIA LOH-HAGAN

*Gods and goddesses were the main characters of myths. Myths are traditional stories from ancient cultures. Storytellers answered questions about the world by creating exciting explanations. People thought myths were true. Myths explained the unexplainable. They helped people make sense of human behavior and nature. Today, we use science to explain the world. But people still love myths. Myths may not be literally true. But they have meaning. They tell us something about our history and culture.*

# 45th Parallel Press

Published in the United States of America by Cherry Lake Publishing
Ann Arbor, Michigan
www.cherrylakepublishing.com

Reading Adviser: Marla Conn, MS, Ed., Literacy specialist, Read-Ability, Inc.
Book Design: Jen Wahi

Photo Credits: ©Howard David Johnson, 2019, cover, 1, 19; ©Andrea Izzotti/Shutterstock, 5; ©Vladimir Melnik/
Shutterstock, 6; ©Artit Wongpradu/Shutterstock, 9; ©Stephen Chung/Shutterstock, 11; ©mountainpix/Shutterstock, 13;
©Scarc/Shutterstock, 14; ©Cody Gregory/Shutterstock, 17; ©Jakub Kyncl/Shutterstock, 21; ©BasPhoto/Shutterstock, 23;
©akimov konstantin/Shutterstock, 24; © Dmitry V. Petrenko/Shutterstock, 27; ©BasPhoto/Shutterstock, 29

45th Parallel Press is an imprint of Cherry Lake Publishing.

Library of Congress Cataloging-in-Publication Data

Names: Loh-Hagan, Virginia, author. | Loh-Hagan, Virginia. Gods & goddesses of the ancient world.
Title: Anubis / written by Virginia Loh-Hagan.
Description: Ann Arbor, Michigan : Cherry Lake Publishing, 2019. | Series: Gods and goddesses of the ancient world | Includes
    bibliographical references and index.
Identifiers: LCCN 2019004127 | ISBN 9781534147737 (hardcover) | ISBN 9781534149168 (pdf) | ISBN 9781534150591 (pbk.) |
    ISBN 9781534152021 (hosted ebook)
Subjects: LCSH: Anubis (Egyptian deity)—Juvenile literature | Mythology, Egyptian—Juvenile literature. | Gods, Egyptian—
    Juvenile literature.
Classification: LCC BL2450.A62 L64 2019 | DDC 299/.312113—dc23
LC record available at https://lccn.loc.gov/2019004127

Printed in the United States of America
Corporate Graphics

## ABOUT THE AUTHOR:

Dr. Virginia Loh-Hagan is an author, university professor, former classroom teacher, and curriculum designer. She wrote a 45th Parallel Press book about morticians. She learned a lot about embalming. She lives in San Diego with her very tall husband and very naughty dogs. To learn more about her, visit www.virginialoh.com.

# TABLE OF CONTENTS

# CHAPTER 1

# JACKAL HEAD OF THE DEAD

*Who is Anubis? What does he do? What does he look like?*

Anubis was an **ancient** Egyptian god. Ancient means old. Egypt is a country in the Middle East. It's in north Africa.

Ancient Egyptians honored Anubis. Anubis was the god of the dead. He's the god of **embalming**. He's believed to have created this process. Embalming is a science. It's the **preserving** of human bodies after dying. Preserving means saving. Embalmers take out body parts. They put special chemicals in bodies. This process keeps bodies from rotting.

For ancient Egyptians, this process made **mummies**.
They dried out dead bodies. They wrapped the bodies.
They believed the wrapped bodies were homes for souls.

It took the ancient Egyptians 70 days to mummify bodies.

A picture of Anubis was drawn on the walls of royal burial sites. He protected the dead.

Ancient Egyptians believed there were 3 types of souls. The Ka stayed in the mummy. The Ba was free to fly in and out. The Akh traveled to the **underworld**. The underworld is the place where dead people's souls lived. It's the world of the dead. The Akh went to the **afterlife**. Afterlife is the life after death.

Anubis ruled the underworld. He ruled over the dead. He guided souls. He led them west. West was the direction of the sunset. That's where the afterlife was.

He's also the god of travelers. He's the god of the lost. He's the god of the helpless. He's the god of orphans. Orphans are people who have lost their parents.

# Family Tree

**Great-grandparents:** Shu (god of light and dry air) and Tefnut (goddess of wet air and rain)

**Grandparents:** Geb (god of the earth) and Nut (goddess of the sky)

**Parents:** Osiris (god of the afterlife, underworld, and rebirth) and Nephthys (goddess of darkness and water)

**Adopted mother:** Isis (goddess of marriage, fertility, motherhood, magic, and medicine)

**Brother:** Horus (god of the sky, kings, and war)

**Wife:** Anput (goddess of burials and mummification)

**Children:** Kebechet (goddess of freshness) and Ammut (eater of hearts)

Anubis always wore black. Black is the color of the Nile River's soil. Soil is the source of life and death. Black is also the color of a mummified body.

Anubis had a human's body. He had a lot of muscles. He had a jackal's head. He had pointed ears. Sometimes, Anubis was just a black dog.

In ancient Egypt, jackals were found around **tombs**. Tombs are places that hold dead bodies. Jackals dug up dead bodies. Ancient Egyptians created Anubis. They thought a powerful dog-god could fight against other dogs. They wanted protection.

 Anubis's animal form was the African golden wolf.

# CHAPTER 2

# A DOG IN THE FIGHT

*Who are Anubis's family members? How does Anubis help Isis and Osiris?*

Osiris, Set, Nephthys, and Isis were powerful gods. They were brothers and sisters. They managed all human matters on earth. They also created many gods. These new gods were also brothers and sisters.

Osiris was the top god. He ruled the world. Set was the god of disorder. Nephthys and Isis were twins. Nephthys was the goddess of darkness. Isis was the goddess of marriage.

The ancient Egyptian gods married their own family members. They did this to keep royal blood in the family. Osiris married Isis. Nephthys married Set. In some stories, Nephthys was unhappy. She loved Osiris. So, she tricked him. She pretended to be Isis. She had a baby with Osiris. That baby was Anubis.

There are different stories about Anubis's father. It could also be Set or Ra.

# All in the Family

Nephthys was an Egyptian goddess. She was the mother of Anubis. She was one of the Great Ennead. The Ennead were the 9 most important gods. They were the first gods. They created the world together. Nephthys was the goddess of darkness and water. She symbolized the death experience. She helped people feel safe as they died. She was known as the Queen of the Embalmer's Shop. She was also known as the "friend of the dead." She sent messages from the living to the dead. She comforted people when their loved ones died. Nephthys had healing powers. She knew magic. She helped pharaohs. She gave pharaohs the power to see "that which is hidden by moonlight." She guarded the Bennu Bird. Bennu lived in the Tree of Life. He was believed to be Ra's soul. Ra was the Sun God.

Sometimes Anubis is shown as a dog next to Isis.

Nephthys didn't want to make Set mad. She **abandoned** Anubis. Abandon means to leave. Anubis became an orphan. Wild dogs helped raise Anubis. They led Isis to Anubis. Isis found Anubis. She adopted him. She raised Anubis as her own. In return, Anubis protected Isis.

Set found out. He was mad. He tricked Osiris. He made a **coffin**. Coffins are cases that hold dead bodies. Set threw a party. He dared Osiris to get in the coffin. Osiris did. Set shut the coffin. He threw it in the Nile River.

Isis searched for Osiris. Osiris floated to sea. He got trapped in a big tree. Isis eventually found him.

Set found out. He hacked Osiris's body into many pieces. He scattered his body parts all over. Isis became a bird. She found most of Osiris's body parts. Anubis helped. He embalmed Osiris. He kept his body from rotting. Anubis also performed **burial rites**. Burial rites are special acts to honor a death.

Isis used magic. She brought Osiris back to life. Osiris was different. He was both alive and dead. He could no longer rule the living world. Anubis stepped aside. He let Osiris become the god of the underworld. He became Osiris's assistant.

 Set was a bad ruler. He brought disorder to the world.

# CHAPTER 3

# DEAD-END JOBS

*What does Anubis do in the underworld? What are his many jobs?*

Anubis had many jobs. Taking care of the dead wasn't easy. He was an embalmer. He made sure the process was done right. He took out organs. Organs were saved in special jars. The organs were protected by different gods. Imset protected livers. Hapi protected lungs. Duamutef protected stomachs. Qebehsenuef protected intestines. Intestines are tubes that carry food out from stomachs.

Anubis sniffed dead bodies. That's why ancient Egyptians stuffed bodies with plants that smelled good. Anubis opened the mummies' mouths. This let dead people eat and speak in the afterlife.

Anubis protected the underworld's gates. He kept souls in. He kept souls out. He served as a judge. He was called the Guardian of the **Scales**. A scale is a tool. It measures things.

Anubis was given Osiris's organs as a gift.

Anubis decided if souls were worthy or not. He determined the fate of souls. Anubis led the souls to the **Hall** of Truth. Hall means great room or house. He took the heart. Hearts were souls. Anubis put hearts on a scale. He measured them against truth. Truth was a feather. Souls heavier than a feather would be eaten. Heavy souls were evil. Souls lighter than a feather could go to the afterlife. Light souls were good. These souls could have an **eternal** life. Eternal means forever.

Anubis guided the good souls. He took them to the afterlife. He took them to Osiris. He held their hands. He made them feel comfortable. He knew people were scared of dying.

Anubis was like a guard dog. He protected tombs. He protected graves. He protected cemeteries. These are places that had

 In some stories, hearts were thrown into a lake of fire.

# Real World Connection

Nicole Chong lives in Singapore. She's one of Singapore's youngest embalmers. She works in her family's funeral business. She started at age 19. She's handled over 600 bodies. She said, "I have always been interested and puzzled at how a body, which has passed on for many days, is able to stay intact." Chong wants to help others. She wants to provide the best care. She wants to give people a good experience with death. She wants to help families feel better.

Rachael Ryan's goal is to be Great Britain's youngest funeral director. She started at age 15. She also learned from her family members. She said, "You could say I was born into it. So the idea of dealing with dead people and comforting their families doesn't faze me. I saw my first body when I was 13. And that didn't worry me."

Most ancient tombs had prayers to Anubis carved on them.

dead bodies. Anubis watched from a **sacred** mountain. Sacred was godly. Anubis punished people who messed with tombs. He sent his army of the dead.

He guarded bodies after they died. He gave ancient Egyptians hope. People were unsure about death. They wanted their souls to be protected.

# CHAPTER 4

# LEADER OF THE PACK

*Who is Anubis's wife? Who are his children?*

Anubis had a wife. Her name was Anput. Anput is the female version of Anubis. Anubis and Anput had a lot in common. They were a good match.

Anput had a woman's body. She had a jackal's head. She's often shown as **nursing** or **pregnant**. Nursing means feeding milk to a baby. Pregnant means having a baby growing inside. Anput was the goddess of funerals. Funerals are special events. They honor people who died. They celebrate people's lives.

In some stories, Anubis married Bastet. Bastet was the goddess of **ointment**. Ointments are healing creams. Bastet helped prepare bodies. She had a woman's body. She had a cat's head.

Anput helped protect Anubis's body.

Both Kebechet and Ammut worked in the Hall of Truth.

Anubis and Anput had a daughter. Her name was Kebechet. Kebechet looked like a snake. She was the goddess of **purification**. Purification means to make clean. Kebechet's name means "cooling water." She was the water used for embalming. She gave water to dead souls while they waited to become mummies. She kept bodies safe from danger.

In some stories, Ammut was also Anubis's daughter. She was a demon. She had a crocodile's head. She had a leopard's body. She had a hippo's back legs. She was known as the "eater of hearts." She ate the hearts of bad souls. These souls died 2 deaths. They were restless forever.

# Cross-Cultural Connection

Xolotl was an Aztec god. Aztecs are ancient people. They lived in northern Mexico. Xolotl had a human body. He had a dog's head. Sometimes, he looked like a monster. Xolotl was the god of death. He was the god of fire and lightning. He was the god of twins. He was the god of sickness. He was the god of bad luck. His main job was to guard the sun. The sun traveled through the underworld every night. Xolotl kept demons away from the sun. His other job was to lead dead people's souls to the underworld. He ran down from heaven. He helped souls cross a deep river. He carried a torch. There's a creation story about him. Xolotl brought bones to the gods. The gods sprinkled their blood on them. The bones became the first humans.

# CHAPTER 5

# BARK OF THE DOG

*What are some stories about Anubis?*

There aren't many stories about Anubis. This is because he was busy. He was the hardest-working god.

But there's a story about Anubis and Set. Set pretended to be a leopard. This happened after he killed Osiris. He wanted to see Osiris's body. He wanted to kill Osiris for good. Anubis protected Osiris. He attacked Set. He put a hot iron on him. This gave Set spots. This is why leopards have spots.

There's another story about Anubis. Anubis was also called the Jackal Ruler of the Bows. The Nine Bows were all the enemies of Egypt. For ancient Egyptians, three meant "many." Nine meant "more than many." Many of the ancient

Anubis was most connected to Osiris's story. Pictured is a statue of Osiris outside a temple.

# Explained By Science

Jackals are wild dogs. They mainly live in Africa and Asia. They mainly live in deserts. They're hunters. They hunt at night. Their bodies are built for hunting. They have curved sharp teeth. They have long legs. They have large feet. They have fused leg bones. Fused means joined. Jackals are made to run fast. They're scavengers. They search for food anywhere. They're not picky eaters. They hang out close to towns. They're often found in cemeteries. They eat dead bodies. They eat rotting meat. They eat leftovers after lions and tigers. Mother jackals throw up food. They feed their vomit to their babies. They do this every few hours. They also eat their own vomit. Scavengers are important. They help nature. They get rid of dead bodies. They break down the material. They poop it out. Their poop is used to grow plants. This is how the food web works.

In ancient Egyptian writings, bows referred to bows and enemies.

Egyptians' enemies fought with bows and arrows. They were from **foreign** lands. Foreign means a different country.

Anubis defeated all of them. He captured the Nine Bows. He tied their arms behind their backs. He guarded them. He mainly helped people. But he also punished them.

Don't anger the gods. Anubis had great powers. And he knew how to use them.

# DID YOU KNOW?

- Anubis is really a Greek name. Anubis's Egyptian name was Anpu or Inpu. Inpu means "to rot." The Greek name became more popular.

- Anubis was known as many things. He was called the First of the Westerners. He was called Lord of the Sacred Land. He was called the Dog Who Swallows Millions. He was called the Master of Secrets.

- Ancient Greeks connected Anubis to Hermes. Hermes was a messenger to the gods. He traveled to the underworld. Some people put them together. They created a new god called Hermanubis.

- In ancient Egypt, male priests took care of dead bodies. They performed rituals. Rituals are series of actions. They're done for special reasons. Priests wore wood masks. These masks looked like Anubis's face.

- Cynopolis was a city in ancient Egypt. It means "city of the dog." People honored Anubis. A burial ground for dogs was found in the city.

- There aren't any temples dedicated to Anubis. Temples are like churches. Anubis's temples were tombs and cemeteries. Scientists found a cemetery of mummy dogs and jackals.

- King Tut's tomb was found in 1922. A statue of Anubis was found. It was made of wood, cement, and gold. It was placed toward the west. This was to help guide King Tut into the afterlife.

- Ancient Greeks and Romans made fun of the Egyptians' animal-headed gods. Ancient Greeks called Anubis "the barker." A popular curse was "by the dog of Egypt."

## CONSIDER THIS!

**TAKE A POSITION!** The Great Ennead are the main Egyptian gods. They're the most important. There are 9 of them. They include Ra, Shu, Tefnut, Geb, Nut, Osiris, Isis, Set, and Nephthys. Should Anubis be in the Ennead? Why or why not? Argue your point with reasons and evidence.

**SAY WHAT?** Read the 45th Parallel Press books about Hades and Hel. These are other rulers of the underworld. Compare them to Anubis. Explain how they're the same. Explain how they're different.

**THINK ABOUT IT!** Morticians are people who take care of dead bodies. They can also be first responders. That means sometimes they're the first to get to disasters. Why is that? Why are morticians important? Would you want to be a mortician? Why or why not?

## LEARN MORE

Braun, Eric. *Egyptian Myths*. North Mankato, MN: Capstone Press, 2019.

Napoli, Donna Jo, and Christina Balit (illust.). *Treasury of Egyptian Mythology: Classic Stories of Gods, Goddesses, Monsters, and Mortals*. Washington, DC: National Geographic Kids, 2013.

Reinhart, Matthew, and Robert Sabuda. *Gods and Heroes*. Somerville, MA: Candlewick Press, 2010.

# GLOSSARY

**abandoned** (uh-BAN-duhnd) left behind

**afterlife** (AF-tur-life) the life after dying, the next world

**ancient** (AYN-shuhnt) old, from a long time ago

**burial rites** (BER-ee-uhl RITES) special acts to honor a death

**coffin** (KAW-fin) a case that holds a dead body

**embalming** (em-BAHM-ing) science or process of preserving human remains by treating with chemicals to keep bodies from rotting

**eternal** (ih-TUR-nuhl) forever

**foreign** (FOR-uhn) from another country

**hall** (HAWL) a house or great room

**mummies** (MUHM-eez) wrapped bodies for embalming

**nursing** (NURS-ing) feeding milk to a baby

**ointment** (OINT-muhnt) healing cream

**pregnant** (PREG-nuhnt) having a baby growing inside

**preserving** (prih-ZURV-ing) saving over time

**purification** (pyoor-uh-fih-KAY-shuhn) the process of cleaning

**sacred** (SAY-krid) godly

**scales** (SKAYLZ) tools used to measure things

**tombs** (TOOMZ) special buildings that hold dead bodies

**underworld** (UHN-dur-wurld) the land of the dead

# INDEX